D1327506

JOINING MATERIALS

IN MY MAKERSPACE

by Rebecca Sjonger

CRABTREE
PUBLISHING COMPANY
WWW.CRABTREEBOOKS.COM

MATTER AND MATERIALS IN MY MAKERSPACE

Author:
Rebecca Sjonger

Series research and development:
Reagan Miller
Janine Deschenes

Editorial director:
Kathy Middleton

Editor:
Janine Deschenes

Proofreader:
Kelly Spence

Design and photo research:
Katherine Berti

Prepress:
Margaret Amy Salter

Print and production coordinator:
Katherine Berti

Photographs:
iStockphoto: p. 6 (pipe cleaners and glue)
All other images by Shutterstock

Library and Archives Canada Cataloguing in Publication

Sjonger, Rebecca, author
        Joining materials in my makerspace / Rebecca Sjonger.

(Matter and materials in my makerspace)
Includes index.
Issued in print and electronic formats.
ISBN 978-0-7787-4620-1 (hardcover).--
ISBN 978-0-7787-4626-3 (softcover).--
ISBN 978-1-4271-2050-2 (HTML)

        1. Materials--Juvenile literature. 2. Materials--Experiments--
Juvenile literature. 3. Engineering--Juvenile literature. 4. Makerspaces--
Juvenile literature. I. Title.

TA403.2.S56 2018   j620.1'1   C2017-907638-8
                                                            C2017-907639-6

Library of Congress Cataloging-in-Publication Data

Names: Sjonger, Rebecca, author.
Title: Joining materials in my makerspace / Rebecca Sjonger.
Description: New York, New York : Crabtree Publishing Company, [2018] |
    Series: Matter and materials in my makerspace | Includes index.
Identifiers: LCCN 2017057958 (print) | LCCN 2018005228 (ebook) |
    ISBN 9781427120502 (Electronic) |
    ISBN 9780778746201 (hardcover : alk. paper) |
    ISBN 9780778746263 (pbk. : alk. paper)
Subjects: LCSH: Materials--Properties--Juvenile literature. |
    Materials--Experiments--Juvenile literature. | Makerspaces--Juvenile literature.
Classification: LCC QC173.36 (ebook) | LCC QC173.36 .S5648 2018 (print) |
    DDC 620.1/1--dc23
LC record available at https://lccn.loc.gov/2017057958

Crabtree Publishing Company

www.crabtreebooks.com   1-800-387-7650

Printed in the U.S.A./032018/BG20180202

Published in Canada
Crabtree Publishing
616 Welland Ave.
St. Catharines, Ontario
L2M 5V6

Published in the United States
Crabtree Publishing
PMB 59051
350 Fifth Avenue, 59th Floor
New York, New York 10118

Published in the United Kingdom
Crabtree Publishing
Maritime House
Basin Road North, Hove
BN41 1WR

Published in Australia
Crabtree Publishing
3 Charles Street
Coburg North
VIC 3058

CONTENTS

YOU CAN BE A MAKER!

Do you learn best by doing hands-on projects? Do you find new ways to reuse everyday items? If so, you could already be a maker! One thing makers do is explore what happens when materials are joined. The Maker Missions in this book will challenge you to join many materials!

A PLACE TO MAKE

Your community may have a **makerspace**. These are places where makers share their skills and supplies. You could also set up one with some friends! Working in a group can lead to new ideas.

No right or wrong!

Makers know that:

- Every new idea can lead a project in unexpected directions.
- Each team member has something great to add to a project.
- Things do not always go as planned. We can learn from the problems we overcome.

4

Makers are people who use teamwork and creativity to solve problems and create new things.

MATTER AND MATERIALS

What do pebbles, paints, and pipe cleaners have in common? They are all made of matter. **Matter is anything that takes up space and has** mass.

MATERIALS

Materials are made of matter. We make some of these materials. Others are found in nature. You will use many materials in your maker projects. Each one has **properties**. These are the characteristics we use to describe materials. Exploring properties will help you choose which materials to work with.

STATES OF MATTER

One property of materials is their **state**. This is the form they take. Two main states of matter are **liquids** and **solids**. Liquids can be poured. They flow into the shape of whatever holds them. Solids keep their shape. They cannot be poured.

liquid

solids

solids

liquid

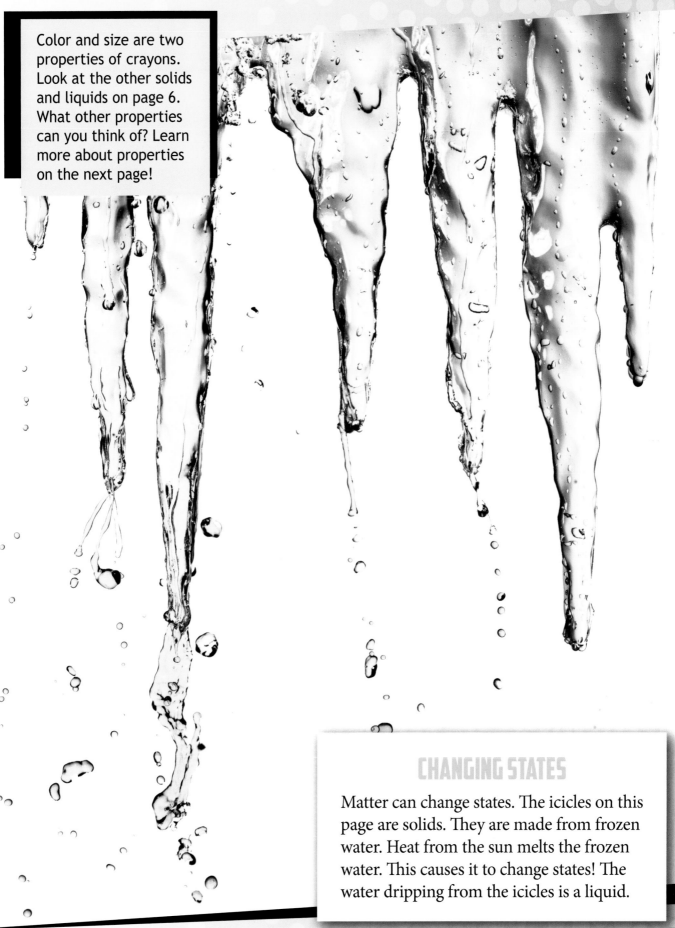

Color and size are two properties of crayons. Look at the other solids and liquids on page 6. What other properties can you think of? Learn more about properties on the next page!

CHANGING STATES

Matter can change states. The icicles on this page are solids. They are made from frozen water. Heat from the sun melts the frozen water. This causes it to change states! The water dripping from the icicles is a liquid.

BE A PROPERTY DETECTIVE

The state of matter is just one of many properties. To explore them, make a list of ways you could describe an object, such as your favorite toy or food. Use your five senses and ask questions. For example:

- What does it look like?
- Could you taste it or smell it?
- Does it make a sound?
- What does it feel like when you touch it?

Ask an adult for permission before you taste or smell any materials, because some can be dangerous.

MADE TO MEASURE

Some properties cannot be explored with your senses. You can find them with tools. For example, you can measure some properties. You could do this with a ruler or a **scale**.

A ruler or a measuring tape can measure how long or tall a material is.

PROPERTY CHALLENGE

Be a property detective! To get started,
explore these properties and materials:

Is it a liquid or a solid?

Is it hard or soft?

What color is it?

Does it bend?

What does its texture feel like?

Is it easy to snap into pieces?

BE A JOINER!

Objects made of joined materials with different properties are all around you. In fact, your body is a mix of solids and liquids! For example, your bones are solids. Your blood is a liquid. Each part joins together. Their properties suit **their purpose.**

GET READY TO MAKE!

Maker projects join all kinds of materials. Like the materials in your body, they must work well together. List their properties to choose which ones to use. Their states are important, too.

Each of your body parts join to help you do everyday activities, such as playing games with your friends.

SEPARATED MATERIALS

Some materials that join to create an object can be **separated**. This means they can be split apart. The separated materials could be made into something else. Other times, the joined parts cannot be separated.

Try it!

Ask an adult for a ballpoint pen that you could take apart. Do you see how it joins solids to hold a liquid? List each material, its properties, and its purpose. Are you able to join the parts back together?

11

MAKER TIPS

Be sure to brainstorm ideas to start each maker project. Give yourself five minutes to come up with as many ideas as possible. Listen to everyone's ideas if you work with a team.

Choose one idea to try. First, plan what you will do. Draw each part and measure your materials. Remember, where you start may not be where your project ends up. Be open to new ideas!

Drum sketch

top

base

string

bottom

Try sketching how your idea will look when it is finished. This step can help you stay focused on the goal!

Help along the way

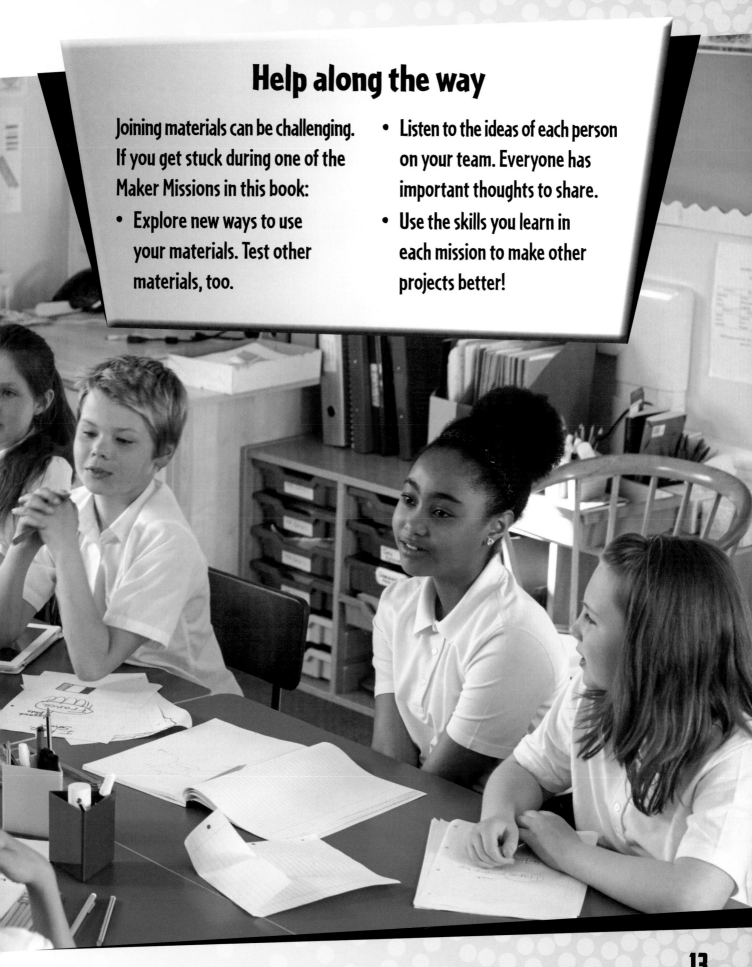

Joining materials can be challenging. If you get stuck during one of the Maker Missions in this book:

- Explore new ways to use your materials. Test other materials, too.

- Listen to the ideas of each person on your team. Everyone has important thoughts to share.

- Use the skills you learn in each mission to make other projects better!

SIMPLE JOINTS

Joining materials can be easy and fun. Grouping solids together is a simple way to create a new object. What could you make by joining sand, driftwood, and seashells? You might build an awesome sand castle! The materials could be separated later to become other objects.

Which materials are joined to make this cool structure?

14

PARTS WITH PURPOSES

Have you ever put together a tent? It is made of many materials that are joined together. Each material has properties that suit its purpose. For example, most tents have a light, fabric cover. Ties or rings join the cover to poles. The poles must be strong enough to hold up the tent. Strong pegs attach to the tent. The pegs hold the tent in place on the ground.

Try it!

A fort is a lot like a tent. Check out the challenge on the next page to try building your own. This is a great project to work on with friends. Share your ideas and have fun testing them!

MAKE A FORT

Join materials to make a fort! It should include a sturdy frame that supports a cover. At least two people must fit inside it.

Materials

- Paper
- Pencil
- Tape measure
- Frame supplies, such as wood, broomsticks, or clothes-drying racks
- Covers, such as newspapers, blankets, or a tarp

THINK ABOUT IT

Design

Will you make your fort indoors or outdoors?

Does the place you choose affect your choice of materials?

Materials

Which properties do your materials need? For example, how strong or long should the supports be? How heavy should the cover be?

Size

How much space do you need?

Why does the size of your cover materials matter?

MISSION ACCOMPLISHED

Did you make a fort that is big enough to fit you and a friend? If not, which materials could you change or add?

Build on what you made! Flip to page 30 for some ideas.

JOINING MATERIALS TOOLKIT

Some materials join other materials to each other. Search your home or school for examples. Look for nails, screws, staples, glue, and tape. What do each of these materials join together to make an object? Which ones hold together hard materials? Which items are best for joining soft materials?

JOINING MATERIALS ALL AROUND!

Check out what you are wearing. What joins the materials in your clothing? Do you see stitches, zippers, laces, or Velcro? These are common joining materials. Even this book is made of joined materials! The pages may be glued or stitched to the cover. How else could you join the parts of a book?

Each joining material has its own properties. They must work with the materials they hold together.

Try it!

Be ready for every project by making your own joining toolkit. Flip to the Maker Mission on the next page to get started. Keep an open mind as you come up with ideas!

GLUE

MAKE IT STAY TOGETHER

MAKER MISSION

Put together your own toolkit of joining materials. Start by exploring ways to join materials. Find at least five ways to join solids, such as cardboard, fabric, or wood. Once joined, you should not be able to pull them apart easily. The five or more joining materials you found make up your toolkit.

Materials

- Paper
- Pencil
- Cardboard
- Fabrics
- Wood
- Scissors
- Elastics
- Paper clips
- Stapler and staples
- Different kinds of tape and glue
- Hammer and nails
- Needles and thread
- Yarn, shoelaces, and rope

THINK ABOUT IT

Materials

How will listing the properties of each solid help you choose a way to join them?

Are there limits to what some of your materials can do?

Design

How will you keep track of what works well and what does not?

Will you test each joining material with each solid? Use your imagination!

Join objects in ways you have never tried before.

MISSION ACCOMPLISHED

Did you find at least five materials that join solids? If not, what other materials could you try? Should you change the solids that you try to join?

After you find at least five joining materials, head to Endless Ideas on page 30.

MAKERS JOIN MATERIALS

Remember, makers explore the properties of materials before joining them. For example, a printmaker joins wood and paper with inks and paints. The first step is choosing solids and liquids to join. Makers look at their textures, sizes, and colors. They see how paints flow and soak into paper.

MAKING MUSIC

Some makers join materials to create music. They explore by blowing on, strumming, or striking materials. Makers test them to find out which sounds they can make. Then they dream up ways to join those materials. Look at the parts of a tambourine. It joins solids that make multiple sounds.

top

base

A drum's base and its top are made of different materials.

Each material in a tambourine is chosen carefully. Some join parts. Others make different sounds!

Try it!

Which materials would you join to make a drum? That's your next challenge! Your project will be a hit if you take some time to plan first.

MAKE A DRUM

Make a drum! Join at least two solids to create your instrument. It must make at least two different sounds when you strike it in different spots.

Materials

- Paper
- Pencil
- Drum base, such as a tin can, old lampshade, or cardboard box
- Drum top, such as a balloon, wax paper, or plastic lid
- Tape, elastics, string

THINK ABOUT IT

Materials

↓

How will experimenting with a variety of materials help you create different sounds?

↓

Will the properties of the base material affect the sounds?

Size

↓

What do you need to measure?

Design

↓

What could happen if the base and top are not held together well?

→ How will you strike your drum to make two different sounds?

↓

Will you use your hands or reuse materials to create drumsticks?

MISSION ACCOMPLISHED

Are you ready to join a band with your drum? If it needs more work, remember to be open to new ideas. Which materials could you try next?

Head to page 30 when you are ready to try a new musical challenge.

25

PARTS AND POSSIBILITIES

Makers love to take apart things and reuse them. Sometimes, they use old or broken materials. When they join old materials to make something new, it is called upcycling.

SAME MATERIALS, NEW OBJECT

Upcycled objects often have different properties, or characteristics, than the old objects that their materials came from. For example, the new object could have a different shape, strength, and weight. The new object often has a new purpose, too. For example, a pile of candy wrappers could become a bag that can carry candy!

Wood from old objects can be upcycled to make new objects, such as furniture.

TRASH TO TREASURE

A world of possibilities is found in the trash, where people often leave broken or old objects. Makers have joined old bike parts to create things such as clocks, lamps, and chairs. The more parts or materials the old object has, the more options you have for the new one.

Try it!

Let your imagination run wild in the challenge on the next page. You will need to brainstorm ideas. Do not give up if things do not go as planned!

REMAKE IT!

Take apart a broken toy and make it into a new object. It must have at least one new property or characteristic that makes it different from the toy. Find ways to join each part together.

Materials

- Paper
- Pencil
- Broken toy
- Hammer
- Screwdrivers
- Scissors
- Joining materials toolkit (see pages 18–21)

DON'T TICK OFF YOUR PARENTS

Always ask an adult for permission before taking apart any objects!

THINK ABOUT IT

Design

Do you want your new object to do a task? Or will it be a piece of art?

Will you brainstorm before or after you take apart your old toy?

Will you come up with ideas for your new object or for each old part?

Materials

Would it be helpful to take note of what each part did before the toy broke?

Size

Which new characteristics, such as size, will your new object have that the old one did not?

MISSION ACCOMPLISHED

Did you join all the parts and make something new that has at least one new property? If you did not succeed, go back to the Maker Tips on page 12 for help. This project may take a while to come together!

When you are ready to make more, go to Endless Ideas on the next page.

ENDLESS IDEAS

Which other materials would you like to try joining? Start by building on the Maker Missions you have already done. Here are some ideas to get you started!

Make it stay together

pages 20–21

- How could your joining materials toolkit help you make a birdhouse, toy boat, or puppet theater?
- What could you reuse to store your toolkit materials?

Make a fort

pages 16–17

- Make it waterproof! Create a cover that keeps liquids from pouring inside.
- Test it by pouring water over your fort—while someone or something is inside it!

Remake it!

pages 28–29

- Would your project improve with more parts? Find more broken toys to join.
- Challenge yourself to join the parts of two or more broken toys.
- Can you join materials to create an object that has more than two new properties?

Make a drum

pages 24–25

- Make more drums in different shapes and sizes to create a set.
- Join different materials to make other musical instruments. What could you join to create a shaker?
- How could you join a liquid and a solid to make music?

LEARNING MORE

BOOKS

Challoner, Jack. *Maker Lab: 28 Super Cool Projects*. DK Children, 2016.

Hirsch, Rebecca. *Properties of Matter*. Cherry Lake, 2012.

Oxlade, Chris. *Joining Materials*. Crabtree, 2008.

Sjonger, Rebecca. *Maker Projects for Kids Who Love Music*. Crabtree, 2016.

• •

WEBSITES

Challenge yourself to build more structures, such as bridges, at:
www.exploratorium.edu/structures

Join materials to make more musical instruments at:
http://pbskids.org/designsquad/build/build-instrument

Learn more about upcycling at:
www.planetpals.com/upcycle_downcycle.html

• •

GLOSSARY

brainstorm To list many ideas—no matter how silly—as quickly as possible

liquid Matter that can be poured and takes on the shape of its container

makerspace A place where makers work together and share their supplies and skills

mass The measurable amount of material in matter

materials Any substance that makes up matter

matter Any material that takes up space and has mass

printmaker A maker who uses materials such as paper and ink to create art

property A characteristic that describes matter

scale A tool that measures an object's weight, or how heavy it is

separate To take apart

solid Matter that does not flow and cannot be poured

state The form that matter takes, such as a solid or a liquid

suit To fit or work well for a certain purpose, or use

texture The look or feel of an object, such as soft or rough

upcycling Making a new object using old or broken materials

INDEX

ABOUT THE AUTHOR

Rebecca Sjonger is the author of more than 50 children's books. She has written numerous titles for the *Be a Maker!* and the *Simple Machines in My Makerspace* series.